Maryland

BY AMY VAN ZEE

The Child's World

Published by The Child's World®
1980 Lookout Drive • Mankato, MN 56003-1705
800-599-READ • www.childsworld.com

ACKNOWLEDGMENTS
The Child's World®: Mary Berendes, Publishing Director
The Design Lab: Design and production
Red Line Editorial: Editorial direction

PHOTO CREDITS: iStockphoto, cover, 1, 3, 7, 9, 10; Matt Kania/Map Hero, Inc., 4, 5; Lonnie Gorsline/Shutterstock Images, 11; Matthew S. Gunby/AP Images, 13; North Wind Picture Archives/Photolibrary, 15; Al Behrman/AP Images, 17; Library of Congress, 19; Richard Thornton/Shutterstock Images, 21; One Mile Up, 22; Quarter-dollar coin image from the United States Mint, 22

LIBRARY OF CONGRESS CATALOGING-IN-PUBLICATION DATA
Van Zee, Amy.
 Maryland / by Amy Van Zee.
   p. cm.
 Includes bibliographical references and index.
 ISBN 978-1-60253-464-3 (library bound : alk. paper)
 1. Maryland—Juvenile literature. I. Title.

 F181.3.V36 2010
 975.2—dc22

                        2010017716

Printed in the United States of America in Mankato, Minnesota.
July 2010
F11538

On the cover:
The Thomas
Point Shoal
Lighthouse is
near Annapolis,
Maryland.

CONTENTS

Geography

Let's explore Maryland! Maryland is in the eastern United States. The Atlantic Ocean is on the state's eastern border.

PENNSYLVANIA

NORTH
WEST
EAST
SOUTH

Appalachian
Mountains

WEST VIRGINIA

MARYLAND

NEW JERSEY

Sharpsburg

Frederick

Baltimore

Fort
McHenry

Gaithersburg

DELAWARE

WASHINGTON, DC

Annapolis

Accokeek

Waldorf

Potomac
River

Salisbury

Ocean City

Saint Mary's
City

Deal
Island

VIRGINIA

Chesapeake Bay

Atlantic
Ocean

Cities

Annapolis is the capital of Maryland. The United States **Naval** Academy is here. Baltimore is the largest city in the state. Frederick and Gaithersburg are other large cities.

Baltimore is sometimes nicknamed "Charm City." ▶

Land

The Chesapeake Bay divides Maryland into two parts. Maryland has **plains** in the east. The central part of the state has rolling hills and valleys. The Appalachian Mountains are in the west. The Potomac River separates Maryland from Virginia.

The Appalachian Mountains extend about 2,000 miles (3,219 km) in the eastern United States. ▶

Plants and Animals

Maryland's state bird is the Baltimore oriole. This bird is orange and dark brown or black. The state flower is the black-eyed Susan. It has yellow **petals** and a black center. The white oak is the state tree.

Black-eyed Susans can be found throughout Maryland. ▶

The largest white oak in the United States was in Maryland. It was almost 100 feet (30 m) tall. It fell during a thunderstorm in 2002.

11

People and Work

More than 5.6 million people live in Maryland. Most of these people live in or near large cities. Maryland is near Washington, DC. Many people work in government jobs there. Others work in **manufacturing** or fishing jobs. Some help the **tourists** who visit the state.

Some people in Maryland package the fish and crabs caught off the state's coast. ▶

QUALITY

13

History

Native Americans have lived in this area for thousands of years. Explorers from Europe came to the area in the 1500s. Later explorers claimed the land for England. More people from England moved to the new land. In the 1700s, these people wanted to be free from England's control. They fought during the **American Revolution**. On April 28, 1778, Maryland became the seventh state of the United States.

Soldiers from Maryland fought the British during the American Revolution. ▶

Maryland was named after Queen Henrietta Maria of England. She was the wife of King Charles I.

Ways of Life

The Preakness Stakes is a famous horse race in Maryland. It is held in Baltimore every May. Fishing, **hiking**, sailing, and other outdoor activities are **popular** in the state. Many people fish for and eat crab. Maryland's cities are home to art, science, and history **museums**.

The Preakness Stakes is held at Pimlico Race Course. Built in 1870, it is the second-oldest racecourse in the United States. ▶

Famous People

John Wilkes Booth was born in Maryland. He shot and killed President Abraham Lincoln in 1865. Frederick Douglass and Harriet Tubman were also born in Maryland. They worked to end **slavery** in the United States.

Harriet Tubman was a slave in Maryland for the first part of her life. ▶

Tubman escaped from slavery in 1849. After this, she helped about 300 other slaves escape to freedom.

Famous Places

Maryland is home to Johns Hopkins University. This school is known for medicine and **research**. Visitors to Maryland can see Fort McHenry. "The Star-Spangled Banner" was written after a battle took place here.

Johns Hopkins University opened in 1876. ▶

State Symbols

Seal

The Maryland state seal shows Lord Baltimore on one side. King Charles I of England gave him the Maryland area in 1632. On its other side, the seal has a farmer and a fisherman. Go to childsworld.com/links for a link to Maryland's state Web site, where you can get a firsthand look at the state seal.

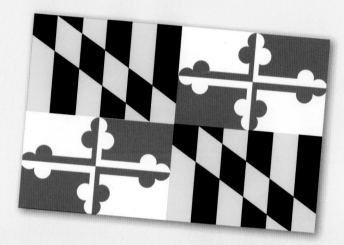

Flag

Maryland's state flag shows two **coats of arms**. They stand for two families that were important in Maryland's history.

Quarter

The Maryland state quarter shows the state capitol in Annapolis. The quarter came out in 2000.

Glossary

American Revolution (uh-MER-ih-kin rev-uh-LOO-shun): During the American Revolution, from 1775 to 1783, the 13 American colonies fought against Britain for their independence. Some people who lived in Maryland fought in battles during the American Revolution.

coats of arms (KOHTS UV ARMS): Coats of arms are shields or other designs that are symbols for families, states, or other groups. Maryland's state seal shows two coats of arms.

hiking (HYK-ing): Hiking is taking a walk in a natural area, such as a hill or a mountain. Many people enjoy hiking in Maryland.

lighthouse (LYT-howss): A lighthouse is a tall building near an ocean or large lake that uses lights to warn ships of danger. The Thomas Point Shoal Lighthouse is along the Chesapeake Bay.

manufacturing (man-yuh-FAK-chur-ing): Manufacturing is the task of making items with machines. Some people in Maryland work in manufacturing.

museums (myoo-ZEE-umz): Museums are places where people go to see art, history, or science displays. People in Maryland visit museums.

naval (NAY-vul): Naval means relating to ships and the navy. The United States Naval Academy is in Maryland.

petals (PET-ulz): Petals are the colorful parts of flowers. The black-eyed Susan's petals are yellow.

plains (PLAYNZ): Plains are areas of flat land that do not have many trees. Maryland has plains in the eastern part of the state.

popular (POP-yuh-lur): To be popular is to be enjoyed by many people. Outdoor activities are popular in Maryland.

research (REE-surch): Research is studying or experimenting on something. Johns Hopkins University in Maryland is known as a place for research.

seal (SEEL): A seal is a symbol a state uses for government business. The Maryland seal has a former king of England on it.

slavery (SLAYV-ur-ee): Slavery is the act of owning a person as property, forcing him or her to do work, and often treating that person badly. Frederick Douglass and Harriet Tubman, who were born in Maryland, worked to end slavery in the United States.

symbols (SIM-bulz): Symbols are pictures or things that stand for something else. The seal and the flag are Maryland's symbols.

tourists (TOOR-ists): Tourists are people who visit a place (such as a state or country) for fun. Tourists come to Maryland to see nature and history.

Further Information

Books

Labella, Susan. *Maryland*. New York: Children's Press, 2005.

Menendez, Shirley. *B is for Blue Crab: A Maryland Alphabet*. Chelsea, MI: Sleeping Bear Press, 2004.

Reynolds, Jeff. *A to Z: United States of America*. New York: Children's Press, 2004.

Web Sites

Visit our Web site for links about Maryland: *childsworld.com/links*

Note to Parents, Teachers, and Librarians: We routinely verify our Web links to make sure they are safe and active sites. So encourage your readers to check them out!

Index